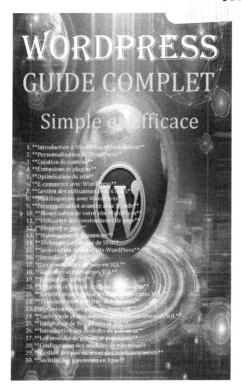

WordPress
COMPLETE GUIDE
Simple and Effective

Introduction

Introducing WordPress Welcome to this WordPress training! WordPress is one of the most popular and powerful content management systems (CMS) in the world. It makes it easy and efficient to create and manage websites, whether you're a beginner or an experienced developer.

Why choose WordPress? WordPress offers incredible flexibility with its themes and plugins, allowing you to customize every aspect of your website. Plus, it's open-source, which means you have access to a vast community of developers and free resources to help you every step of the way.

This training is designed to guide you through all the steps of creating and managing a professional WordPress site. Whether you want to start a blog, a portfolio, or an online store, this book will provide you with the knowledge and skills you need to succeed.

Chapter 1: The Basics of WordPress

WordPress History WordPress was launched in 2003 by Matt Mullenweg and Mike Little as an open-source content management system. Since then, it has become the most widely used CMS in the world, powering more than 40% of websites. Its success is based on its ease of use, flexibility and active community.

Installing WordPress Installing WordPress is a simple process that can be done in just a few steps:

1. Download WordPress from the official website (wordpress.org).
2. Unzip the downloaded file and transfer the content to your server via FTP.
3. Create a MySQL database for WordPress on your server.
4. Launch the WordPress installer by accessing your domain through a web browser.
5. Follow the on-screen instructions to set up your site (site name, database credentials, etc.).

WordPress User Interface Once WordPress is installed, you will be greeted by the dashboard, the main user interface. Here are some key elements of the dashboard:

1. **Dashboard** : Overview of your site, with quick links to important sections.
2. **Articles** : Manage blog posts, add, edit, and delete.
3. **Pages** : Management of your site's static pages.

4. **Appearance** : Customizing the look and feel of your site through themes and widgets.
5. **Extensions** : Install and manage extensions to add functionality to your site.

Chapter 2: Customizing WordPress

WordPress Themes Themes determine the look and layout of your WordPress site. There are thousands of free and paid themes available. To install a theme:

1. Go to **Appearance** > **Themes** in the dashboard.

2. Click Add to search for new themes.
3. Once you've found a theme you like, click Install, then **Activate** to use it on your site.

Customizing Themes After installing a theme, you can customize it to match your brand. Here's how to do it:

1. Go to **Appearance > Customize**.
2. Use the available options to change colors, fonts, logos, backgrounds, and more.
3. View changes in real-time and click **Publish** to save them.

Using widgets and menus Widgets and menus allow you to further customize your site by adding functionality and organizing navigation.

1. **Widgets** : Go to **Appearance > Widgets**. Widgets can be added to different areas of your theme (sidebars, footers, etc.) to display content such as calendars, categories, searches, and more.
2. **Menus** : Go to **Appearance > Menus**. Create and organize navigation menus to improve the user experience on your site. You can add pages, posts, categories, custom links, and more.

Chapter 3: Content Creation

Content Types (Pages, Posts) WordPress allows you to create two main types of content: Pages and Posts.

1. **Pages** : Pages are used for static content, such as "About", "Contact", etc.
2. **Articles** : Articles are used for dynamic content, such as blog posts. They can be categorized and labeled.

Using the Gutenberg Editor Gutenberg is the default content editor for WordPress. It uses blocks to facilitate the creation of rich and dynamic content.

1. To add a post or page, go to **Posts > Add** or **Pages > Add**.
2. Use the editor to add blocks of text, images, videos, quotes, and more.
3. Each block can be customized individually (font size, background color, etc.).

Adding media (images, videos)

1. To add images or videos, click **Add Media > Block** in the Gutenberg Editor.
2. Upload files from your computer or choose from the media library.
3. You can adjust the settings for each media (size, alignment, caption).

Chapter 4: Extensions and Plugins

What is an extension? An extension (or plugin) is an add-on that adds functionality to your WordPress site. There are thousands of free and paid extensions available, offering features ranging from SEO to security, image galleries, and social media integration.

Installing and managing extensions

1. To install an extension, go to **Extensions > Add** from the dashboard.
2. Use the search bar to find a specific extension or browse recommended extensions.
3. Click Install **Now** to add the extension to your site.
4. Once the installation is complete, click Enable to start using the extension.

Here are some popular and must-have plugins to improve your site's performance, security, and management:

1. **Yoast SEO** : Improve your site's SEO with easy-to-use SEO tools.
2. **Akismet Anti-Spam** : Protect your site from unwanted comments and spam.
3. **Jetpack** : A set of tools to improve social media security, performance, and management.
4. **WooCommerce** : Turn your WordPress site into a full-fledged online store.
5. **Wordfence Security** : Add an extra layer of security with a firewall and protection against malicious attacks.

Chapter 5: Site Optimization

SEO for WordPress Search engine optimization (SEO) is essential for improving your site's visibility on search engines like Google. Here are some tips for optimizing your WordPress site:

1. **Use optimized titles and descriptions** : Make sure that each page and post has a catchy title and a relevant meta description.
2. **Include keywords** : Incorporate relevant keywords into your titles, descriptions, and content without overdoing it.

3. **Optimize images** : Use descriptive file names and add alt tags to images.
4. **Create quality content** : Regularly publish relevant, high-quality content that meets the needs of your visitors.
5. **Use SEO extensions** : Extensions like Yoast SEO can help you optimize your pages and posts.

Performance and security The performance and security of your site are crucial to providing an optimal user experience and protecting your data.

1. **Reduce image size** : Compress your images to reduce your site's load time.
2. **Use a cache** : Install a cache extension like W3 Total Cache to improve your site's performance.
3. **Update regularly** : Make sure WordPress, your themes, and plugins are always up to date for the latest security improvements and fixes.
4. **Use an SSL certificate** : An SSL certificate encrypts the data between your site and visitors, enhancing security and improving SEO.
5. **Back up regularly** : Use backup extensions like UpdraftPlus to back up your site regularly and prevent data loss.

Backup and Restore Regular backups are essential to protect your site from data loss and errors. Here's how to backup and restore your WordPress site:

1. **Install a backup extension** : Extensions like UpdraftPlus or BackupBuddy make it easy to back up your site.
2. **Schedule automatic backups** : Configure the extension to perform automatic backups at regular intervals.
3. **Store backups remotely** : Keep your backups on cloud storage services like Google Drive, Dropbox, or a remote server.
4. **Restore a backup** : If necessary, use the extension to restore your site from a previous backup.

Chapter 6: E-commerce with WordPress

Introduction to WooCommerce WooCommerce is the most popular extension for turning a WordPress site into a full-fledged online store. It offers a multitude of features to manage products, orders, payments, and much more. WooCommerce is flexible and can be customized to meet all your e-commerce needs.

Setting up the online store To set up your online store with WooCommerce, follow these steps:

1. **Install WooCommerce** : Go to **Extensions >
   Add**, search for WooCommerce, install and
   activate the extension.
2. **Setup Wizard** : Use the WooCommerce Setup
   Assistant to set up basic settings such as your
   store location, currencies, payment methods,
   and shipping options.
3. **Customize WooCommerce Pages** :
   WooCommerce automatically creates pages for
   the store, cart, checkout, and customer
   account. You can customize these pages by
   going to **Appearance > Customize >
   WooCommerce**.

Product and order management

1. **Add Products** : To add a product, go to
   Products > Add. Fill in the product information
   such as name, description, price, images, and
   categories.
2. **Manage Products**: Use the **Products** section to
   view all products, edit them, delete them, and
   manage inventory.
3. **Manage Orders** : Go to **WooCommerce >
   Orders** to see all orders received, update their
   status, and process payments.

Conclusion

We went through the basics of WordPress, from installing and customizing it, to creating content and adding plugins. We've also covered optimizing your site for search engines and security, as well as setting up an online store with WooCommerce.

Chapter 7: Managing Users and Roles

Adding and managing WordPress users makes it easy to collaborate by adding multiple users. To add a user:

1. Go to **Users > Add** from the dashboard.
2. Fill in the required fields (username, email address, password).
3. Assign a role to the user from Admin, Editor, Author, Contributor, or Subscriber.
4. Click **Add User** to finalize.

Understanding roles and permissions Each user role has specific permissions:

1. **Administrator** : Full access to all site features and settings.
2. **Publisher** : Can publish and manage posts and pages, including those of other users.
3. **Author** : Can publish and manage their own articles only.
4. **Contributor** : Can write articles but cannot publish them.
5. **Subscriber** : Can manage their profile and read subscriber-only content.

Advanced user management For specific needs, you can use extensions like Members or User Role Editor to create custom roles and adjust the permissions of existing users.

Chapter 8: Multilingualism with WordPress

Setting up a multilingual site To create a site that is accessible in multiple languages, you can use dedicated extensions:

1. **WPML** : A premium plugin for translating every element of your site, including themes and plugins.

2. **Polylang** : A free extension with basic features to manage a multilingual site.

Content translation

1. Install and activate the extension of your choice.
2. Configure the languages available in the extension's settings.
3. Translate your posts, pages, categories, and other elements by adding versions in each language.

Translation management Multilingual plugins allow you to manage translations directly from the WordPress interface. You can also collaborate with translators to ensure the quality of the translations.

Chapter 9: Advanced Customization with Code

Customizing Your Theme To further customize your theme, you can add CSS and PHP code:

1. **Custom CSS** : Go to **Appearance > Customize > additional CSS** to add custom CSS code and change the style of your site.
2. **PHP Changes** : For more advanced edits, edit your theme's files in **Appearance > Theme Editor.** Be careful to always create a child theme to avoid losing your changes during updates.

Add functionality with code

1. Use the `functions.php` file to add custom functions to your theme.
2. You can add shortcodes, custom content types, and much more using PHP.

Chapter 10: Monetizing Your WordPress Site

Advertising and Affiliate Programs

1. **Google AdSense** : Display Google AdSense ads to generate revenue based on your site traffic.
2. **Affiliate programs** : Participate in affiliate programs to recommend products and services, and earn a commission on sales generated through your links.

Create and sell digital products

1. Use WooCommerce to sell digital products such as ebooks, online courses, and software.
2. Set up secure payment options and manage downloads of purchased products.

Premium Content and Memberships

1. Create premium content that is only accessible to paid members.
2. Use extensions like MemberPress or Restrict Content Pro to manage memberships and restricted access.

Chapter 11: Using Page Builders

Introduction to Page Builders Page builders are powerful tools that allow you to create complex layouts without having to write any code. Some of the most popular ones include Elementor, Beaver Builder, and Divi.

Elementor

1. **Installation** : Install and activate Elementor from **Extensions > Add**.
2. **Usage** : Open a page or post, then click Edit with **Elementor**.
3. **Features** : Use drag-and-drop widgets to add columns, sections, images, videos, buttons, and more.

Beaver Builder

1. **Installation** : Install and activate Beaver Builder.
2. **How to use** : Open a page or article, then click **Page Builder**.
3. **Features** : Use Beaver Builder's modules to create custom and professional layouts.

Chapter 12: Advanced Blogging

Content Strategies

1. **Editorial planning** : Establish a release schedule to ensure a regular posting frequency.
2. **Keyword research** : Use tools like Google Keyword Planner to identify relevant keywords to target in your articles.
3. **Headline Optimization** : Write catchy, SEO-optimized headlines.

Reader engagement

1. **Comments** : Encourage readers to leave comments and respond to them to build an active community.
2. **Social Media Sharing** : Add share buttons to make it easy for readers to share your articles.
3. **Newsletters** : Use tools like Mailchimp to create newsletters and let your subscribers know about new posts.

Chapter 13: Maintenance and Troubleshooting

Regular maintenance

1. **Updates** : Keep WordPress, themes, and plugins up to date to get the latest features and security fixes.
2. **Backups** : Schedule regular backups to prevent data loss.
3. **Database cleanup** : Use plugins like WP-Optimize to clean and optimize your database.

Common troubleshooting

1. **Common errors** : Resolving 404 errors, database connection errors, and block editor errors.
2. **Debug Mode:** Enable debug mode in the `wp-config.php` file to identify technical issues.
3. **Support and Assistance** : Use WordPress support forums and community groups for help.

Chapter 14: Advanced SEO Techniques

Optimisation on-page

1. **Title tags and meta descriptions** : Use relevant and persuasively written keywords.
2. **User-friendly URLs:** Use clear and descriptive permalinks.
3. **H1, H2, H3 tags** : Structure your articles with hierarchical title tags.

Optimisation off-page

1. **Backlinks** : Create quality backlinks by collaborating with other websites.
2. **Social media** : Use social media to promote your content and attract visitors.
3. **Guest content** : Write guest posts for popular blogs in your niche.

Chapter 15: Securing Your WordPress Site

Basic Security

1. **Strong passwords** : Use strong passwords for all user accounts.
2. **Two-factor authentication** : Enable two-factor authentication to add an extra layer of security.

3. **Security extensions** : Install extensions like Wordfence or Sucuri to protect your site from malicious attacks.

Security Monitoring

1. **Logs** : Track changes to your site with logging extensions.
2. **Security Notifications** : Receive real-time alerts in the event of a security threat.
3. **Security audits** : Conduct regular audits to verify the security of your site.

Chapter 16: Introduction to SQL

What is SQL? SQL (Structured Query Language) is a standardized language used to interact with relational databases. It allows you to create, read, update, and delete data in a database. SQL is used by many database management systems (DBMS) such as MySQL, PostgreSQL, SQLite, and SQL Server.

Why learn SQL? SQL is a key skill for many developers and database administrators. It is used in a variety of contexts, from website management to data analysis. Mastering SQL allows you to efficiently manipulate and query data stored in relational databases.

Relational databases Relational databases store data in the form of tables, which are collections of rows and columns. Each table represents an entity, and relationships between tables are established by keys. Key features of relational databases include:

1. **Structured schema** : Data is organized into tables with columns defined by a schema.
2. **Referential integrity** : Relationships between tables are maintained by foreign keys.
3. **Standardization** : Data is standardized to reduce redundancy and improve data integrity.

Chapter 17: Basic Commands in SQL

Select data

1. **SELECT** : The SELECT command is used to retrieve data from a database.

```
SELECT * FROM table_name;
```

This command selects all columns in the specified table.

2. **WHERE** : Use WHERE to filter results based on specific conditions.

```
SELECT * FROM table_name WHERE condition;
```

For example, to select rows where the age column is greater than 30:

```
SELECT * FROM table_name WHERE age > 30;
```

Insert data

1. **INSERT INTO** : The INSERT INTO command is used to add new rows to a table. `INSERT INTO table_name (column1, column2) VALUES (value1, value2);` For example, to insert a new record with the values John and Doe :`INSERT INTO table_name (first_name, last_name) VALUES('John', 'Doe');`

Update data

1. **UPDATE:** The UPDATE command is used to modify existing data in a table.`UPDATE table_name SET column1 = value1 WHERE condition;` For example, to update the first name of a specific record: `UPDATE table_name SET first_name = 'Jane' WHERE last_name = 'Doe';`

Delete data

1. **DELETE** : The DELETE command is used to delete data from a table.`DELETE FROM table_name WHERE condition;` For example, to delete all lines where the first name is John :`DELETE FROM table_name`

```
WHERE first_name = 'John';
```

Chapter 18: SQL Functions and Operators

Aggregation functions

1. **COUNT** : Count the number of rows in a table.

```
SELECT COUNT(*) FROM table_name;
```

2. **SUM** : Calculate the sum of a column.

```
SELECT SUM(column_name) FROM table_name;
```

3. **AVG** : Calculate the average of a column.

```
SELECT AVG(column_name) FROM table_name;
```

4. **MAX** : Find the maximum value for a column.

```
SELECT MAX(column_name) FROM table_name;
```

5. **MIN** : Find the minimum value of a column.

`SELECT MIN(column_name) FROM table_name;`

SQL operators

1. **Comparison operators** : Used to compare values.
   a. = : Equal to
   b. <> : Different from
   c. > : Greater than
   d. < : Less than
   e. >= : Greater than or equal to
   f. <= : Less than or equal to
2. **Logical operators** : Used to combine conditions.
   a. AND : Both conditions must be true.
   b. OR : At least one of the conditions must be true.
   c. NOT : Inverse la condition.
3. **Arithmetic operators** : Used to perform mathematical operations.
   a. + : Addition
   b. - : Subtraction
   c. * : Multiplication
   d. / : Division

Chapter 19: Joining Tables

Introduction to joins Join is used to combine rows of two or more tables based on a common column. They are used to retrieve related data that is scattered across different tables.

Types of joins

1. **INNER JOIN** : Returns rows that have matching values in both tables.

```
SELECT columns FROM table1 INNER JOIN table2
ON table1.column = table2.column;
```

2. **LEFT JOIN** : Returns all rows in the left table, and the corresponding rows in the right table.

```
SELECT columns FROM table1 LEFT JOIN table2
ON table1.column = table2.column;
```

3. **RIGHT JOIN** : Returns all rows in the table on the right, and the corresponding rows in the table on the left.

```
SELECT columns FROM table1 RIGHT JOIN table2
ON table1.column = table2.column;
```

4. **FULL JOIN** : Returns all rows when there is a match in one of the tables.

```
SELECT columns FROM table1 FULL JOIN table2
ON table1.column = table2.column;
```

Chapter 20: Creating and Managing Databases

Create a database

1. **CREATE DATABASE** : Creates a new database.`CREATE DATABASE database_name;`

Create tables

1. **CREATE TABLE** : Creates a new table in a database.`CREATE TABLE table_name (`
       `column1 datatype,`
       `column2 datatype,`
       `...`
   `);`

Edit tables

1. **ALTER TABLE** : Modifies an existing table (add column, delete column, etc.).`ALTER TABLE table_name ADD column_name datatype;`

Delete tables and databases

1. **DROP TABLE** : Deletes an existing table.

`DROP TABLE table_name;`

2. **DROP DATABASE** : Deletes an existing database.

```
DROP DATABASE database_name;
```

Chapter 21: Advanced Security for SQL Databases

Access control and permissions

1. **GRANT** : Grant specific permissions to
   users.GRANT SELECT, INSERT ON
   database_name.table_name TO
   'user_name'@'host';

2. **REVOC** : Revoke specific user
   permissions.REVOKE SELECT, INSERT ON
   database_name.table_name FROM
   'user_name'@'host';

Data Security

1. **Data encryption** : Use SQL functions to encrypt
   sensitive data.SELECT AES_ENCRYPT('data',
   'key');

2. **Audit and logging** : Implement auditing mechanisms to track user activities and detect suspicious behavior.

Chapter 22: Transactions and Data Integrity

Transactions

1. **BEGIN, COMMIT, ROLLBACK** : Use transactions to ensure that database operations are executed atomically.BEGIN;
UPDATE table_name SET column_name = value WHERE condition;
COMMIT;

Data integrity

1. **Constraints** : Use constraints to ensure data integrity.
    a. **PRIMARY KEY** : Ensures that each row in a table is unique.
    b. **FOREIGN KEY** : Maintains relationships between tables.
    c. **CHECK** : Imposing conditions on the data entered.

Chapter 23: Optimizing SQL Performance

Indexing

1. **Create indexes** : Use indexes to speed up queries.`CREATE INDEX index_name ON table_name (column_name);`

Query Analysis

1. **EXPLAIN** : Analyze SQL queries to identify bottlenecks.`EXPLAIN SELECT * FROM`

```
table_name WHERE condition;
```

Query optimization

1. **Working with views** : Simplify complex queries by using views.CREATE VIEW view_name AS SELECT column_name FROM table_name WHERE condition;

Chapter 24: Backing Up and Restoring SQL Databases

Data backup

1. **mysqldump** : Use tools like mysqldump to back up your database.mysqldump -u user_name -p database_name > backup_file.sql

Data Restoration

1. **Importing backups** : Restore a database from a backup file.mysql -u user_name -p database_name < backup_file.sql

Chapter 25: WordPress and SQL Integration

Connecting WordPress to the Database

1. **wp-config.php**: Configure the database connection information in the `wp-config.php` file.

```
define('DB_NAME',
'database_name');
define('DB_USER', 'user_name');
define('DB_PASSWORD', 'password');
define('DB_HOST', 'localhost');
```

Interact with WordPress Database

1. **wpdb** : Utilisez la classe wpdb pour exécuter des requêtes SQL dans WordPress.`global $wpdb;`

```
$results = $wpdb->get_results("SELECT *
FROM {$wpdb->prefix}table_name WHERE
condition");
```

Chapter 26: Introduction to Payment Modules

What is a payment module? A payment module is an extension or service that allows online payments to be processed on your website. It supports different payment methods, like credit cards, PayPal, and bank transfers. It is essential for any e-commerce site, as it facilitates transactions and ensures the security of user data.

Why use a payment module? The use of a payment module offers several advantages:

1. **Security** : Payment modules are designed to secure transactions and protect user information.
2. **Convenience** : They make the checkout process easier for customers, improving the user experience.
3. **Simplified management** : They allow you to track and manage payments directly from your WordPress dashboard.

Chapter 27: Popular Payment Modules

WooCommerce Payments

1. **Introduction** : WooCommerce Payments is the official WooCommerce extension for accepting payments on your site.
2. **Installation** : Install and activate WooCommerce Payments from Extensions > **Add.**
3. **Setup** : Follow the setup wizard to connect your bank account and set up payment options.
4. **Features** : WooCommerce Payments supports credit cards, Apple Pay, and more.

PayPal

1. **Introduction** : PayPal is one of the most popular and widely accepted online payment services.
2. **Installation** : Install and activate WooCommerce PayPal Checkout from **Extensions > Add.**
3. **Setup** : Connect your PayPal account and set up payment options.
4. **Features** : Accept PayPal, PayPal Credit, and credit card payments.

Stripe

1. **Introduction** : Stripe is an online payment platform known for its flexibility and powerful features.

2. **Installation** : Install and activate WooCommerce Stripe Payment Gateway from **Extensions > Add**.
3. **Setup** : Connect your Stripe account and set up payment options.
4. **Features** : Credit card acceptance, Apple Pay, Google Pay, and more.

Chapter 28: Setting Up Payment Modules

Configurer WooCommerce Payments

1. **Installation** : Go to **Extensions > Add** and search for WooCommerce Payments. Install and activate the extension.
2. **Login** : Follow the instructions to connect your bank account to WooCommerce Payments.
3. **Settings** : Configure currencies, accepted payment options, and transaction settings. Make sure that all security options are enabled to protect user data.

Set up PayPal

1. **Installation** : Go to **Extensions > Add** and search for WooCommerce PayPal Checkout. Install and activate the extension.

2. **Login** : Connect your PayPal account to the extension by following the steps in the setup wizard.
3. **Settings** : Configure payment options, currencies, and transaction settings. PayPal also offers advanced options for managing payments and refunds.

Configure Stripe

1. **Installation** : Go to **Extensions** > **Add** and search for WooCommerce Stripe Payment Gateway. Install and activate the extension.
2. **Login** : Connect your Stripe account to the extension by following the instructions provided.
3. **Settings** : Configure payment options, currencies, and transaction settings. Stripe offers great flexibility and many options to customize the payment experience.

Chapter 29: Managing Payments and Refunds

Payment tracking

1. **WooCommerce Dashboard** : View payments received, pending orders, and recent

transactions from the WooCommerce dashboard.

2. **Reports** : Use WooCommerce reports to analyze sales, revenue, and performance of your online store. Detailed reports can help you identify trends and make informed decisions.

Reimbursement management

1. **Refund requests** : Manage refund requests directly from the WooCommerce dashboard. Make sure to respond quickly to customer inquiries to maintain customer satisfaction.

2. **Refund process** : Make refunds through the configured payment modules (WooCommerce Payments, PayPal, Stripe, etc.). Follow the steps specific to each module to ensure proper processing.

3. **Refund Policy** : Establish a clear refund policy and communicate it to your customers. A transparent policy helps to avoid misunderstandings and build trust with your customers.

Chapter 30: Security of Online Payments

Security measures

1. **SSL/TLS** : Make sure your site uses an SSL/TLS certificate to encrypt payment data. This ensures that sensitive information, such as credit card numbers, is transmitted securely.
2. **PCI DSS** : Comply with PCI DSS security standards to protect credit card information. Payment Card Industry Data Security Standard (PCI DSS) is a security requirement for businesses that process card payments.
3. **Secure information** : Use tools and extensions to monitor and secure transactions. For example, extensions like Wordfence or Sucuri can add an extra layer of protection to your site.

Security Extensions

1. **Wordfence** : Use Wordfence to add an extra layer of security to your site. This extension offers features such as firewalls, security scans, and real-time alerts.
2. **Sucuri** : Use Sucuri to monitor and protect your site from security threats. Sucuri offers a full

range of security services, including protection against malware, DDoS attacks, and security breaches.